Heman R. Timlow

A Discourse Occasioned by the Death of Abraham Lincoln

Heman R. Timlow

A Discourse Occasioned by the Death of Abraham Lincoln

ISBN/EAN: 9783337372279

Printed in Europe, USA, Canada, Australia, Japan

Cover: Foto ©Thomas Meinert / pixelio.de

More available books at **www.hansebooks.com**

A DISCOURSE

OCCASIONED BY THE DEATH

OF

ABRAHAM LINCOLN,

PRESIDENT OF THE UNITED STATES.

DELIVERED AT RHINEBECK, N. Y., APRIL 19, 1865,
AT A PUBLIC DEMONSTRATION OF THE CITIZENS,

BY
REV. HEMAN R. TIMLOW.

———

Rhinebeck, N. Y.
1 8 6 5 .

RHINEBECK, April 20, 1865.

REV. AND DEAR SIR,—

The undersigned, in compliance with the unanimous wish of the community, respectfully solicit the manuscript of your discourse, delivered yesterday, on the occasion of the death of our late President, for publication.

H. DeLAMATER,
J. M. KEESE,
ALFRED DRURY,
W. B. PLATT,
E. M. SMITH,
ALFRED WELCH.
G. C. LANSING, and others.

RHINEBECK, April 20, 1865.

H. DeLAMARTER, &c.

GENTLEMEN,—

Agreeably to request, I submit the manuscript of my discourse to your disposal. It is due to myself to state that it was prepared in a few hours. Nor have I felt at liberty to revise it. With the exception of a few verbal corrections it is precisely as written. I am conscious that full justice has not been done the distinguished subject. It is only as a tribute (feeble indeed) to departed worth, that I consent to its publication. The service of Wednesday was, in the strictest sense, a *union* service. Neither Party nor Denomination, as such, intruded. I felt myself to be the mouthpiece of a stricken and mourning community. Under this feeling I wrote and delivered the discourse. If I have succeeded in expressing the public estimate of the lamented dead to any satisfying degree, it will be to me one of the best compensated labors of my life.

Let us ever hold in grateful remembrance the name of ABRAHAM LINCOLN.

Ever yours,
HEMAN R. TIMLOW.

DISCOURSE.

It is a dark cloud beneath which we meet to-day.

Its presence overwhelms us.

The weight at our heart is crushing.

It is not merely a conventional summons that has called together this sorrowing multitude. A grief, keen as a personal bereavement—mourning, bitter as that of Rachel for the children that were not, distinguish this assembly. With a nation, we share a mysterious and awful sorrow. It came with the unexpectedness and suddenness of a thunderbolt from the cloudless heavens.

And there is that in this sorrow that adds immeasurably to its poignancy and stuns with unwonted horror. We mourn, not only as when twice before the Head of the Republic was removed by death: Allied to this terrible event is an act of such atrocity, that to give it a fitting record language is too poor. The genius of our institutions, the type of our civilization, the culture of the age, the popular sentiment, are so averse to such a savage spirit, that the thought of its prevalence is too abhorrent to be enter-tained. We can only account for it by re-ferring it to that school of wickedness in which a large portion of our land has been educated to carry on the causeless and dis-astrous revolt that has well nigh rent us in twain. In other countries such acts are not unfamiliar. History is full of them. And we read them with comparative indifference. But to-day we mourn the infamy that will forever stain a page in our history. As if high treason, the easy perjury of high offi-cials, insult to the nation's ensign, the ini-tiation of a war of brethren, the slaughter of a half million of men, the perpetration of the cruelties of Libby, Andersonville, and Salisbury, as if all *these* were not enough to fill the cup of the Republic's humiliation and all shame! To this must be added a crime that approaches in its enormity that of the Judæan Judas Such a crime has shocked this great nation throughout its vast extent. The popular heart is thrilled to its inmost fibre.

It staggers faith to believe all this real; but, alas! *it's too real, too real.*

In the weakness and despondency to which our natures are given, we at first feel that we cannot drink this cup. Were it not for that blessed truth, never so radiant and comforting as now, "The Lord omnipotent reigneth," we could not drink it; but in the darkness and gloom of the hour, the teachings of our holy religion come in to dis_pel every repining thought, and turn the heart above the spirit of sweet surrender, "even so Father, for so it seemed good in thy sight." We *do* believe that God in per_mitting this sad event "has done all things well." With a truthful, hopeful spirit, we "kiss the rod that smites." "Shall not the judge of all the earth do right?"

O, how appalling the intelligence borne to us on swift wing four days ago, that our beloved President was dead; and when the circumstances of his death were narrated, dumbness for a time seized the masses.— Spontaneously the store, the shop, the fields were vacated. The pressure upon the heart was so great as to check every impulse of business. Men gathered in public places as if seeking for sympathy. At times it was impossible to realize the dreadful fact. It seemed rather that each had awakened out of a frightful dream. And the few days that have since elapsed find us but little better prepared to realize the event. It still seems but a troubled dream.

And yet the President is dead. O, how hard the task to write on this paper, the word *dead*. The Providence of God has permitted the event, and we now must write and mourn him dead. It is because he is dead, that we are here to-day. His body does not lie before us. But still *he is here,* for he has a home in every heart. Yes, we bear him about with us in our hearts   And this will be no less a funeral service than if his "mortal remains" were here.

At the seat of Government, at this very hour, loving hearts are conducting his funeral obsequies. There, are assembled Envoys from abroad, Cabinet Ministers, Senators, Magistrates, the great and good from all parts of the land. But these constitute not the chief mourners. Thousands are there of the toiling masses of the country, to honor the memory of one lifted from among them to the highest position of trust, in their power to confer. And there are mourners there to-day such as have never before congregated at the funeral of a Chief Magistrate. The multitudes of "freed men," whose simple-worded prayer "God bress Massa Lincoln," has often ascended to Heaven for him they counted their deliverer, are there and mourn him as a father lost. And were it possible, there would to-day be one vast funeral procession of all races, reaching from the Aroostook hills to the golden shores of the Pacific. But as all cannot assemble in our National Capital, it has been appropriately recommended that everywhere fitting services should be held, and such honors paid as the feelings of every community might prompt.

But once before in our history has there been such a spectacle as is now presented. But one American before, has ever had so deep a hold upon the affections and confidence of the people. Washington will hold the first place in the hearts of his countrymen. Next to him stands our beloved Lincoln. It is touching and impressive to behold the nation throbbing as one heart at this event. However rancorous have been party spirit and strife, these are now buried, and one universal wail of sorrow is heard. All now concede this high place to the departed President; with one consent the highest honors are paid him.

When we place Abraham Lincoln in the rank we have assigned him, it is not intended to disparage other statesmen who have

faithfully served their generation and country. With pride do we recall their names.
Many of them possessed talents of an order
so high that neither Washington or Lincoln
can be classed with them. But these two
men were raised up by God to act in particular crises of the country's history. As pa-
triots and rulers they well fulfilled their
trusts. They are thus prominent because
of these crises and the fidelity with which
they met them.

We may for a little time inquire for the
secret of that character and life and service
that so endeared our late President to his
countrymen, and that now calls forth such
signal demonstrations of grief over his death.
Such an inquiry will disclose the greatness
of the loss we sustain, and vindicate the pro-
found sorrow universally prevailing.

With the main facts of his life you are already familiar. Any lengthy detail of these
would only be tedious. From his birth, Feb.
12th, 1809, until his entrance upon public
life, but little occurred in his history to dis-

tinguish him from ordinary pioneer life.—
Less than a year was spent at school. But
he was undergoing a training in the hands
of Providence, that neither schools or books
could effect. In his obscure home and oc-
cupation he was developing vigorously in
body and mind It cannot be doubted, that
there he was maturing that physical strength
that was needful to sustain him in the try-
ing duties of the past four years. While de-
prived of advantages for acquiring knowl-
edge, his thirst for it was unconquerable.—
We read of his walking seven or eight miles
to borrow an English Grammar. When
not at labor he was reading the few books a
western settlement in those days afforded.
Among these were Pilgrim's Progress, Esop's
Fables and Ramsey's life of Washington.—
In tracing his future career, we follow him
on his flat-boat excursions, working with
the axe, engaged in surveying, keeping a
store, in village debates, serving in Black
Hawk's war, until in 1836 we find him ad-
mitted to the bar. After this he was sever-

al times sent by his constituents to represent them in the State Legislature. He succeeded well in his profession. In 1846 he represented his district in Congress.— Very soon after we find him the representative of the anti-slavery sentiment in his State. In the convention of 1856 that nominated John C. Fremont for President, he received one hundred and two votes for the Vice-Presidency. Before this he was but little known at the East. He was introduced to the Eastern and Middle States by a speech he delivered in New York City, Feb. 27th, 1860. The following May he was nominated for the Presidency by the Republican Party, and elected in November He was re-elected Nov. 1864.

Some of the more important incidents of his life and administration will appear as we attempt to analyze his character and acts.

It is a more difficult task to give an analysis of Mr. Lincoln's character than at first appears. He is of that class of men who have not specially marked traits that separate them from others. Most public men possess some one trait that is distinguishing. One excels as an orator, another as a reasoner, another as an economist, another in those qualities that constitute a successful diplomatist. But in Mr. Lincoln we discern no single quality of mind that is prominent above others. What Mr. Irving says of Washington may very appropriately be said of Mr. Lincoln; his character "may want some of those poetical elements which dazzle and delight the multitude, but it possessed fewer inequalities, and a rarer union of virtues than perhaps ever fell to the lot of one man. Prudence, firmness, sagacity, moderation, an overruling judgment, an immovable justice, courage that never faltered, patience that never wearied, truth that disdained all artifice, magnanimity without alloy."

There was that *simplicity and transparency* of character in Mr. Lincoln that makes it impossible to define it. *He was a man to whom we could get nearer* than any other public man of his generation. In this fact we see an element of his greatness. Nothing about him was disguised, and every one saw him just as he was. Whatever were his weaknesses or virtues, all plainly appeared. It was this evident openness and candor that commended him to the unreserved confidence of the nation. Just so far as the people saw him they relied upon him, and *they saw all of him.* Not a shadow of concealment or affectation was ever detected.

Implied in this idea of simplicity and transparency is that of the most unquestionable honesty of motive and purpose. If we except the occasional passionate utterances of a heated campaign, it was rare to find any one who would dispute his entire honesty of character. Whatever errors of policy might be imputed to him, were not attributed to improper motives, but only to defects of judgment.

And in connection with this integrity of heart was a singleness of purpose that will ever dignify his name. From the time of his first inaugural address until he fell in unconsciousness by the bullet of the assassin, he had in mind but one object, and that was to restore and maintain the constitutional union of the States. A candid study of his course must persuade the most skeptical that such was the governing desire and a m of his heart. His famous letter to Mr. Greely, and other public papers, explicitly affirm this. And his conduct was in harmony with such words.

He has sometimes been spoken of as undecided and vacillating in his policy. Friends as well as foes have charged this. But instead of such a charge being well grounded in fact, there is the most indubitable testimony to his *independence* and *firmness.*— Facts could be indefinitely multiplied in support of this. But I shall be content to quote from a journal, a most resolute opposer of Mr. Lincoln's administration, whose witness will be confessed to be valuable as being that of an opponent.* This paper says: "He has given a signal proof of a strong and manly nature in the fact, that although he surrounded himself with the most considerable and experienced statesmen of his party, none of them were able to take advantage of his inexperience, and gain any conspicuous ascendency over him.

"All his chief decisions have been his own; formed indeed after much anxious and brooding consultation, but in the final result, the fruit of his own independent volitions. He has changed or retained particular members of his cabinet, and endorsed or rejected particular dogmas of his party, with the same ultimate reliance on the decisions of his own judgment. It is this feature of his character, which was gradually disclosed to the public view, together with the cautious and paternal cast of his disposition, that gave him his strong and increasing hold on the

*New York World, April 17.

confidence of the masses." This estimate I believe to be perfectly just.

And *the sterling common sense* of the man, out of which flowed that good judgment that has made so many of his public acts memorable, should be noticed. Considering the vast number of official appointments to be made, extending to thousands, he must have the credit of acting a judicious part. One need but glance at the civil, military and naval lists, to learn what a demand is made upon sound discretion to fill them. It was utterly impossible for him to examine in detail the qualifications, antecedents and recommendations of every applicant or appointee. To a large degree he must rely upon the opinion of others. And yet with quick discernment he sifted these opinions and reached his own conclusions. Had he entirely relied on the judgment of others, Grant, Sherman, Schofield and other skillful generals had been in retirement.

Nor is his judgment less remarkable with respect to political and military measures.

He was not hasty in adopting a policy.—
Entering as an inexperienced man upon the
most responsible duties ever laid upon a ruler, and assuming office at a crisis when the
counsels of the wisest statesmen were in-
definite and contradictory, he indicated his
good sense in awaiting the developement of
events. The cry from the radical press was,
"wanted, a policy." Had this demand been
satisfactorily met, I have no hesitation in
affirming that to-day the Union would have
been in fragments. The paper already quot-
ed speaks on this wise, and I think justly :
"Had Mr. Lincoln started with his emancipation policy in the spring of 1861, his administration would have been wrecked by
the moral aid which would have been given
to the South by the northern conservatives,
including a large part of the Republican
party. Had he refused to adopt the emancipation policy much beyond the autumn of
1862, the Republican party would have refused support to the war, and the South
would have gained independence by their

aid * * * * * Regarding the growth of
opinion simply in the light of a *fact*, we
must concede that Mr Lincoln's slowness,
indecision and changes of policy, have been
in skillful or at least fortunate adaptation
to the prevailing public sentiment of the
country."

The same good judgment has appeared in
his correspondence with state officials, and
likewise in his delicate intercourse with for-
eign nations. To what extent we are in-
debted to his calmness and wisdom and sagacity, cannot now be definitely ascertained.
But we are persuaded that to his moderation and firmness we in a good measure owe
our peaceful relations abroad.

Mr. Lincoln thoroughly understood his
position as President of the United States.
From the first he assumed only to be *the
servant of the people.* The capacity to perceive the exact relations he sustained to the
people, and a resolute purpose to execute
the popular will, are marked features of his

character. "Know thyself," was the laconic inscription on the Delphic temple. This wise injunction of antiquity found itself fulfilled in the person of our departed President. His biographer says of him in his younger days: "He had talked with men who were regarded as great, and he did not see where they differed so much from others. He reasoned probably, that the secret of their success lay in the fact of original capacity and untiring industry. He was conscious of his own powers. He was a logician and could not resist logical conclusions. If he studied, *why* might not *he* achieve ?"

Whatever in after life was laid upon him to do, he *tried* to do, and succeeded. When he became President, he saw that as this government rested on the consent of the governed, and was supported by the popular sentiment, it was necessary to consult and follow what was evidently the will of the people. Hence it was, that fault was found with him, that he was not more of a *leader*. But this he could not consistently be. He was simply the servant of the opinion already formed. He could move only so fast as public opinion sustained him. As has already been said, his emancipation proclamation had been fatal to the harmony of the North if issued a year earlier. Just at the fitting time to avoid the successful opposition of the enemies of the measure and fully satisfy its friends, he gave it to the nation.

And this estimate of his official relations, together with his simplicity and transparency of character, brought him into most familiar and sympathetic communion with the people. They saw him just as he was.— What he said, was couched in language too plain to be misunderstood. What he did, had the rich savor of honesty that commanded their confidence. And his gentle, loving nature, his generous impulses and genial social qualities won their hearts. O, how the people who knew him and appreciated his qualities of mind and heart, loved Abraham Lincoln.

Notwithstanding he was ruler of the most

powerful nation on the face of the earth, he never assumed to be more than the humblest American citizen. He was one of the people, and they loved him. *You* loved him, my friends. Did you not? Did you ever love a public servant more? Tell me, ye who are old, and remember when the nation mourned Washington, and who remember the death of all the Presidents, tell me, since Washington's day, has one been so greatly loved, as our own Lincoln? Did one ever die so lamented?

He was simple hearted as a child. So kind was he, that he once said, on a public occasion, he had "never knowingly planted a thorn in any one's breast." Maligned, the subject of pitiless ridicule, belied, called traitor, tyrant, despot, and all the hard names malice could devise, he never returned to such an unkind word. He had to a high degree the spirit of our Divine Lord, of whom it is said, "when he was reviled, reviled not again." Could such a heart fail to sympathize with the people? And is it possible for any to be insensible to such exhibitions of kindness and forbearance and forgiveness?

And how forcibly this spirit presents itself in all his later history. Not only did he offer sympathy to his brethren of the North, but even to his misguided and revolting subjects of the South. Read his messages and find if you can one word, breathing hatred toward those in rebellion. How dignified all his utterances. How vivid the contrast of his messages and proclamations with those emanating from the make-believe president at Richmond!

Could he have lived to become truly known by his Southern subjects, he would have been as tenderly loved by them, as he has been fiercely hated. They would have found him their most devoted friend. A significant passage occurs in one of the bulletins of the Secretary of War announcing his death, to the effect, that in Cabinet meeting on Friday he *spoke kindly of Gen.*

Lee. And so he felt toward even the stoutest rebel.

O yes : that dear man, now enshrouded in the vestments of the grave, was ever in closest, tenderest sympathy with all his fellow-men.

And this fact, my friends, calls to mind that other trait, which will be his chief honor in history, *his love of liberty.* You have no doubt agreed with me in all that I have said concerning him. Upon this subject so near and dear to the noble President's heart, there are contrary views. Some of you have honestly disagreed with him. You have not perhaps disagreed upon abstract principles so much as upon practical measures. With the heart we have attributed to him, you can readily see that he must have had a great interest in the condition and destiny of the African in our country.

In his public speeches and debates he has abundantly acknowledged the Constitutional difficulties in the way of the speedy and general deliverance of the bondsmen. After the present troubles were far advanced, he still disclaimed the right to effect what his heart had long desired and prayed to be effected. But at last that time came which John Quincy Adams long years ago affirmed to be the legitimate time, and which Providence had hastened. In the exercise of a right which he believed to be conferred upon him as the Commander-in-Chief of the Army and Navy, and for purely military purposes, he issued the memorable proclamation that decreed liberty to 3,000,000 slaves.

Now, I say it was just like Abraham Lincoln to do this thing. But few men would have had the courage to do it in the face of the opposition manifested. He felt it to be right and just, and *he did it.*

We may oppose the measure as unconstitutional or inexpedient. This each one has a right to do. But in history its author will ever be identified with it, and his name will be radiant with the honor and glory of having struck the chains from the African bondsmen in this land. His administration will hereafter be signalized as inaugura'ing the final and decisive measure for removing this stain from our country. He was the proper man to do it. Through him has the dragon been slain. It is now in its death-throes. It still had strength, through an emissary trained for the hellish work, to martyr its destroyer. O, what would not this curse of slavery do to perpetuate itself! What has it not done? And to finish the awful tragedy of evils, it acts the assassin's part, and sacrifices to its vengeance the grand old Hero of Freedom. He was permitted to live long enough to lead his country and the "emancipated hosts" to the borders of their Caanan of Liberty. As from some Pisgah, he gazed and saw the promised land ; but, like the Patriarch of old, he was not permitted to enter. He had led them through the sea and wilderness. His work was done. His work was *well* done. We mourn that such an honored, useful life could not have ended according to the order of nature. But God's ways are not our ways. We humbly bow in submission.

There is much in the career of Abraham Lincoln, to constitute a model and encouragement for the American youth. Recall his humble origin, the poverty against which he struggled, his lack of advantages for education, his want of social position and influential friends, and who upon these can base any reasonable hope that this young man will rise to the first place in history? But roused by the consciousness that what others have done he could do, animated by an honorable ambition, carried on by an irresistible energy, cherishing noble purposes and with a resolute determination to make the most of himself, it is not long before, in his life, appear those prophecies of future usefulness and position, that the past few years have fulfilled.

By discreet and upright deportment, he secured the confidence of all with whom he came in contact. When persuaded as to the righteousness of a given course, he could not be diverted from it. He was governed by high principle. I believe it is impossible to cite a single instance in his public career, wherein he ever consciously sacrificed a sense of right. Unlike many statesmen, he never sacrificed general principles to a transient expediency. By his fidelity to the True, the Right, the Good, he gained not only favor and applause, but, what is better than all, LOVE.

Such a character and life, and such success, is worthy of study and imitation by every youth. Particularly are these of vast encouragement to those unblest with worldly goods. Such is the nature of our political institutions, that no door of promotion is closed to any. Industry, economy and a becoming life, can overcome the obstacles that poverty or obscurity, that adversity and friendlessness may interpose to advancement. The life of Abraham Lincoln is ample proof of this. He is a natural and noble product of this country and its institutions. It is not a little singular, nor a slight

matter of gratulation to Americans, that
the two men ranking highest in our government should have risen from the humblest
walks of life.   Mr. Lincoln's successor, like
himself, (under Providence) is "the archi-
tect of his own fortune."   Because of such
examples we ought indeed to cherish and be
thankful for political institutions that yield
such fruits.

How far Mr. Lincoln's religious character
may be held up as a model, I cannot confi-
dently say.   It is to be regretted that ~~so~~
~~few of~~ our public men exert so little *direct*
influence upon the church.   But that our
late President was a Christian man I believe.
His peculiar structure of mind, would for-
bid any very special demonstrations of religious feeling.   It would rather appear in
all his acts, impressing upon them a glow
and beauty that were otherwise unattaina-
ble.   His outward life is universally admit-
ted to be blameless.   As far as the outward
can be taken as an expression of the in-
ward life, I think we can trace in him a de-

vout christian spirit. When about to leave
his quiet home at the West for assumption
of his high office at Washington, in conscious weakness and with touching modesty
he besought his fellow townsmen to pray for
him. Often since he has publicly express-
ed his fullest reliance upon God. Often has
he directed the nation in her darkest hours
of history to Him who is Head over all and
King for evermore. To friends, in unreserved private intercourse, he has spoken definitely upon the matter of personal salvation.
It has been my privilege to converse with
several who have communicated thus with
him. They have gone from his presence,
persuaded that he was an humble Christian.

He is known to have been a man of prayer. He leaned not upon his counsellors of
earth, as he did upon the Infinite Counsel-
lor. I frankly confess that he lacked some
things that are *popularly* considered tests
of a christian character. But my friends,
such a life of reverent unfaltering trust in
God, such a love of Truth, such a prayerful

spirit, such conscientious fidelity to duty, such devotion to whatever he knew to be right, such self abnegation, are much upon which to base a judgment. Simple assent to a creed and public profession, without these, are nothing; but *these* without such assent and profession, are every thing before God.

With the abatement of what Mr. Lincoln has concealed concerning his interior religions life, I would commend him as a model to young men before me. His good name, his many virtues, his success, the confidence and love he won, are your possible inheritance. Follow him as far as he followed Christ.

The death of Mr. Lincoln has subjected our Government to an unlooked for and most thorough test. This is an important matter for us to consider. Already in these years of war had we as a nation undergone almost every possible trial. God has been proving us before the world. Other nations supposed our form of government unsound and weak, and from the first predicted our downfall. We have successfully encountered every storm. The most terrible ordeal of any government is an internal convulsion—a revolution. Well may despotism survey in speechless wonder the spectacle this country presents! But now as if to apply the final test, behold a conspiracy is permitted by violence and blood, to strike down the Head of the Government. What would be the effect of such an act in France? What nation of Europe would not reel under such a blow? But under our system, however great the shock to the hearts of the people, the Government feels it not. Not the first thought of insecurity arises in the mind. And if the Vice President and Cabinet Ministers had fallen (as we feared was the great object of the conspirators) there would still remain a stable government. The *people* would still remain, and speedily other public servants would be chosen to take the place of the lamented dead. It does seem to me, that this dreadful visitation has

bee permitted by God, to exhibit still further the strength of our institutions. By it
he further tests us. It will be overruled for
the good of Freedom. Henceforth, may
the oppressed millions of the other continent appeal in greater confidence to the
despotic power that holds sway over them.
And the champions of larger liberties for
the people of England and on the Continent,
may now without any restraint press the
claims of those they represent. Thus may
the unnatural death of our beloved Chief
Magistrate subserve most important ends
for Freedom.

But I have already detained you too long.
It is my desire simply to guide your thoughts
so that the occasion may be profitably im-
proved. The lessons to be learned are many.
The warnings given most impressive. The
more obvious of these will occur to your
minds without special mention.

Our beloved President is dead. As oft
as the sad fact comes before the mind, the

appaling circumstances appear in vivid array.

But I have not the heart to speak of the manner of his death. There is nothing in the history of tragic horror that surpasses it. Such an end for any man, however humble in life, or even were he vile, would shock and overpower us. But to have our Chief Magistrate, and *such* a Magistrate, so warm in the cause of the country, so loyal to God and Humanity, so full of concern and sympathy for the people, so pure in life, so true to friend and magnanimous to foe, so illustrious in the virtues that dignify and adorn human life, and in whom so many hopes were centered, to have *him* terminate such a career of glory by the hands of *such* an assassin, pierces the heart with keenest agony.

But, my friends, let us turn from the terrible tragedy. Think not too much on it least passion secure the mastery. It is no time to indulge feelings of vengeance at the grave of him we so bitterly mourn. It is for us to copy the spirit of the slain chief who never failed to forgive his enemy.

I know it is very hard to suppress angered and even vengeful emotions that rise. If the assassin were really in our hands, and we in excitement of passion, who would answer for his life? Let us remember we live in a Christian land and age. It is our duty and privilege to exercise a Christian spirit. This spirit pays respect to law and order. We have representatives commissioned to try and judge the criminal and execute justice. My prayer is, that all implicated in this bloody work may be overtaken by the sword of Justice; but let the proper authorities wield that sword. Cherish only becoming thoughts of Justice, and nothing of personal vengeance. "Vengeance is mine and I will repay saith the Lord." God will avenge his own. His retributive justice slumbers not. We will leave the criminal and all his fellow-conspirators in the hand of God, allowing no fires of passion to burn within us.

We will rather come and kneel by the coffin of our dear departed President, and try to catch his spirit. At his side we would learn. When with us in life he taught us much, and now being dead, he yet speaketh. His great mind and heart still preside over the nation. He is not lost to us.

Wiser and happier will the country be because he lived. From his administration dates a new era in our history. He was God's chosen instrument to conduct the nation through the furnace appointed for purification. In every way was he adapted for this. Him no bribe could buy. Him no terror could affright. Him no reverse could discourage or dismay. Him no good work could weary. He was confident in his cause, and confident in God, because he believed his cause just. His faith in the principles of our government and his trust in the people were marvellous. His heart never beat one pulsation of suspicion or distrust of these.

If the voice of the people had been consulted, Abraham Lincoln had not died. It was the prevailing desire to have him live, and reap some results of his stupendous work during the past four years. But God appointed otherwise. And strange the permission of Providence in the place and manner of his death. Not in Richmond, whither two weeks ago we followed him with beating heart, but in his own Capital. Not in his chamber in the stillness and darkness of midnight, but in an illuminated public place and before hundreds of spectators. Not by disease or accident, but by the dastard hand of violence.

Never did widow and orphan have greater sympathy. Your hearts, my brethren, are full of sorrow for her so suddenly bereft of such a husband. O how sadly stricken she: Pray for supporting grace and that she may realize, "Thy Maker is thy husband." And pray that the sons, old enough to perceive and copy the honored father's excellences, may walk in his steps and shed lustre on the name that it is now such a distinction to bear.

Nor can we fail to remember in fervent prayer, the present incumbent of the sadly vacated office. Well may Andrew Johnson tremble to assume his responsibilities. To follow Abraham Lincoln were not easy. But wisdom and grace may be his to give him strength for his duties. May the God of wisdom abundantly qualify him for the work he has to do. God in mercy save him from violence and preside over his administration and crown it with success.

Let the prayer also ascend for the distinguished Secretary of State, upon whose life ruffian hands were also laid, but which failed in fully executing the bloody deed. May he be spared to resume the functions of his office, and give his counsels in the important crisis now upon us. And may his assistant be raised up to health. His is a life too full of promise to be cut down thus early. But God's will be done. The blessing of restoration too, rest on all stricken under that roof.

And may the Providence from whose eye no man can escape, and who has said, "Be sure your sin will find you out," guide our authorities in their efforts to discover the extent and parties of this awful conspiracy, that the innocent may be relieved from suspicion, and the guilty be brought to justice, the majesty of law and order be vindicated.

God bless our common country, and speedily introduce the reign of Peace. May the union of the States be restored and perpetuated for evermore. May the Republic be restored to more than former splendor, the laws be everywhere respected, brotherly love universally prevail. May Heavenly wisdom preside in the adjustment of our difficulties, the ends of justice be secured, the people preserved in moderation, unbroken harmony be preserved to the nation through the ages. The grace of God banish all malice, injustice and the spirit of strife, encourage forbearance and a generous charity.

President Lincoln is dead. What pangs shoot through the heart at this announcement! Considering his importance to the nation, we are almost led to say, "would that I had died for thee" We little knew how much we loved him, till he was taken from us How near he was to us! We feel that no stranger has died, but a household friend, at once brother and father Some of us saw the President's benignant face, as he paused among us for a moment on his way to the seat of Government. And can we ever forget it?

No! we will never forget thee, dear one, no, *never.* Here in the heart thou shalt ever live. Oft will we commune one with the other, and talk of thy virtues and deeds. We will tell them to children, and children's children. Side by side with the illustrious Washington, we lay thee in our hearts.—Thus enshrined by the American people, no higher earthly honor can be thine.

And we desire that thy tomb shall be somewhere under the shades of Mt. Vernon, so that when patriot pilgrims visit the sanctuary of the dead where reposes "the Father of his Country," they shall also stand by the grave of him, who shall hereafter be held in grateful veneration, as the Martyr of Liberty in 1865.

Peace be to thy ashes.

www.ingramcontent.com/pod-product-compliance
Lightning Source LLC
Chambersburg PA
CBHW021559270326
41931CB00009B/1302